# STARBOY

**Bukayo Saka** is one of the **finest** young footballers in the world right now.

The awesome **Arsenal** attacking player has been lighting up the **Premier League** with his silky skills since 2019 and is a crucial player for **England.**

*YOU LOVE SAKA. WE LOVE SAKA . . .*

# FOOTBALL SUPERSTARS

# SAKA

## RULES

SIMON MUGFORD          DAN GREEN

# CONTENTS

CHAPTER 1 – **STARBOY** ............................................................5

CHAPTER 2 – **EALING KID** ......................................................13

CHAPTER 3 – **SCHOOL STAR** ...............................................25

CHAPTER 4 – **SAKA'S HEROES** ............................................37

CHAPTER 5 – **YOUNG GUNNER** ...........................................43

CHAPTER 6 – **THE SAKA LIFE** ..............................................55

CHAPTER 7 – **YOUNG LION** ...................................................63

CHAPTER 8 – **BUKAYO'S BREAKS** .......................................71

CHAPTER 9 – **TAKING OFF** .....................................................83

CHAPTER 10 – **HEROES AND HEARTBREAK** .....................89

CHAPTER 11 – **RISING STARS** ..............................................99

CHAPTER 12 – **PREMIER CLASS** ........................................107

# SAKA
## RULES

> *Hi,* pleased to meet you.

> We hope you enjoy our book about Bukayo Saka!

> I'm **VARbot** with all the facts and stats!

WELBECK

SIMON    DAN

Published in 2023 by Welbeck Children's Limited,
part of the Welbeck Publishing Group
Offices in: London - 20 Mortimer Street, London W1T 3JW &
Sydney - Level 17, 207 Kent St, Sydney NSW 2000 Australia
www.welbeckpublishing.com
Text © 2023 Simon Mugford
Design & Illustration © 2023 Dan Green
ISBN: 978-1-80453-573-8

**Writer:** Simon Mugford
**Designer and Illustrator:** Dan Green
**Design Manager:** Sam James
**Senior Commissioning Editor:** Suhel Ahmed
**Production:** Arlene Alexander

A catalogue record for this book is available from the British Library.

Printed in the UK
10 9 8 7 6 5 4 3 2 1

**Statistics and records correct as of May 2023**

## Attacking

Incredibly good at pushing forward into space.

## Creativity

Uses flair and intelligence to create goal-scoring opportunities.

## Flexibility

Saka can play on either wing, at the back or as an attacking midfielder.

## Control

Excellent first touch and the ability to move play on.

## Passing

You can rely on Saka to play a killer ball.

## Goals and assists

Simply one of the best in the business – and he's a **TOP LAD**, too!

## SAKA IS QUICKLY BECOMING ONE OF THE WORLD'S *ELITE* ATTACKING PLAYERS

# THE SAKA STATS

These are the numbers that show what an **AWESOME** player Saka is.

**37** goals and . . .

**40** assists in . . .

**178** matches for **Arsenal**

**8** goals and . . .

**7** assists in . . .

**26** **England** appearances.

**1** FA CUP WIN

**1** England Men's Player of the Year Award

**2** Arsenal Player of the Season Awards

**£97.5 MILLION**

transfer value

# SAKA I.D.

**NAME:** *Bukayo Ayoyinka T. M. Saka*

**NICKNAME:** *Starboy / Little Chilli*

**DATE OF BIRTH:** *5 September 2001*

**PLACE OF BIRTH:** *Ealing, London, England*

**HEIGHT:** *1.78 m*

**POSITION:** *Right winger / midfielder*

**CLUBS:** *Arsenal*

**NATIONAL TEAM:** *England*

**LEFT OR RIGHT-FOOTED:** *Left*

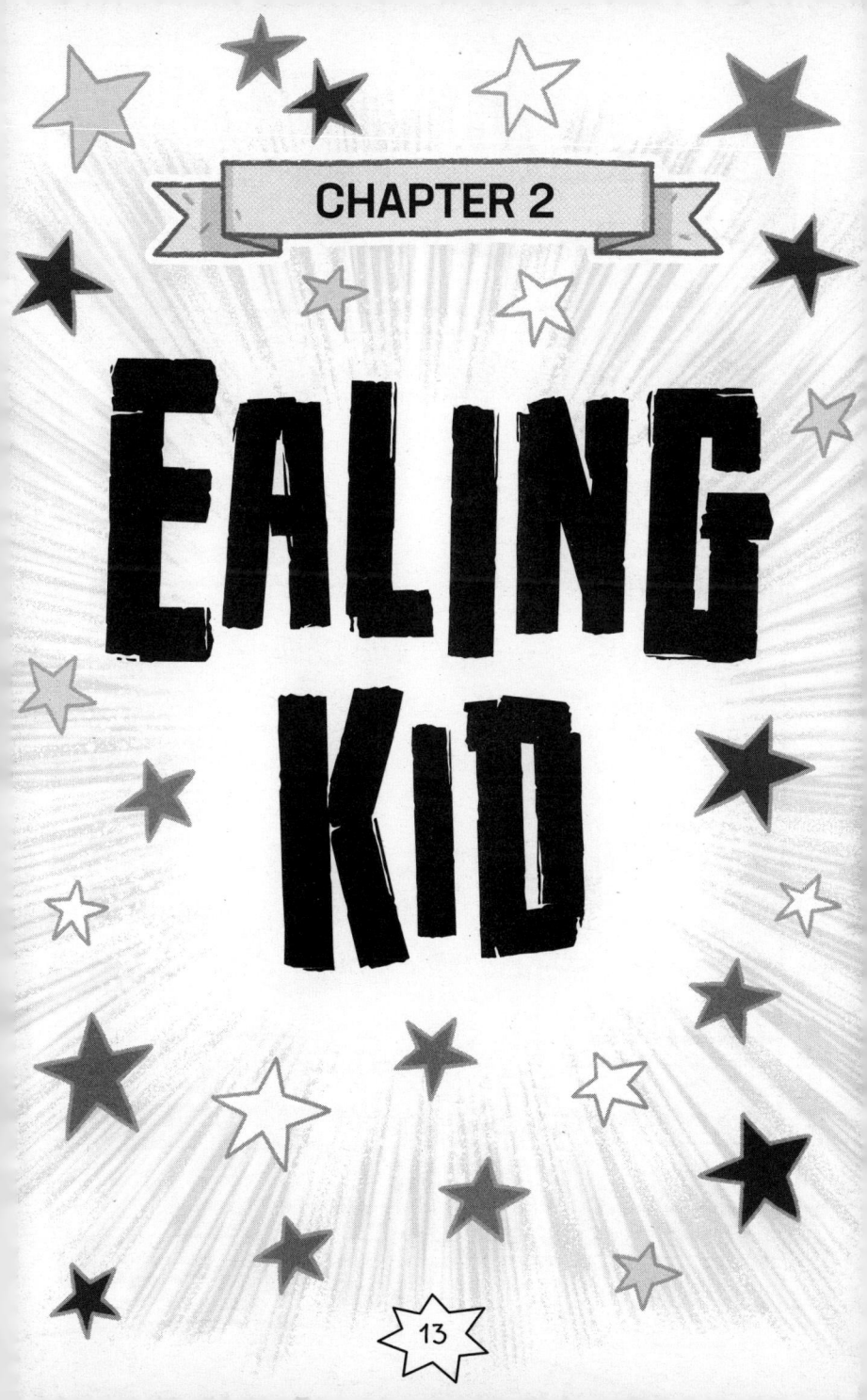

CHAPTER 2

EALING KID

**Bukayo Saka** was born in Greenford, in **Ealing, West London,** in 2001.

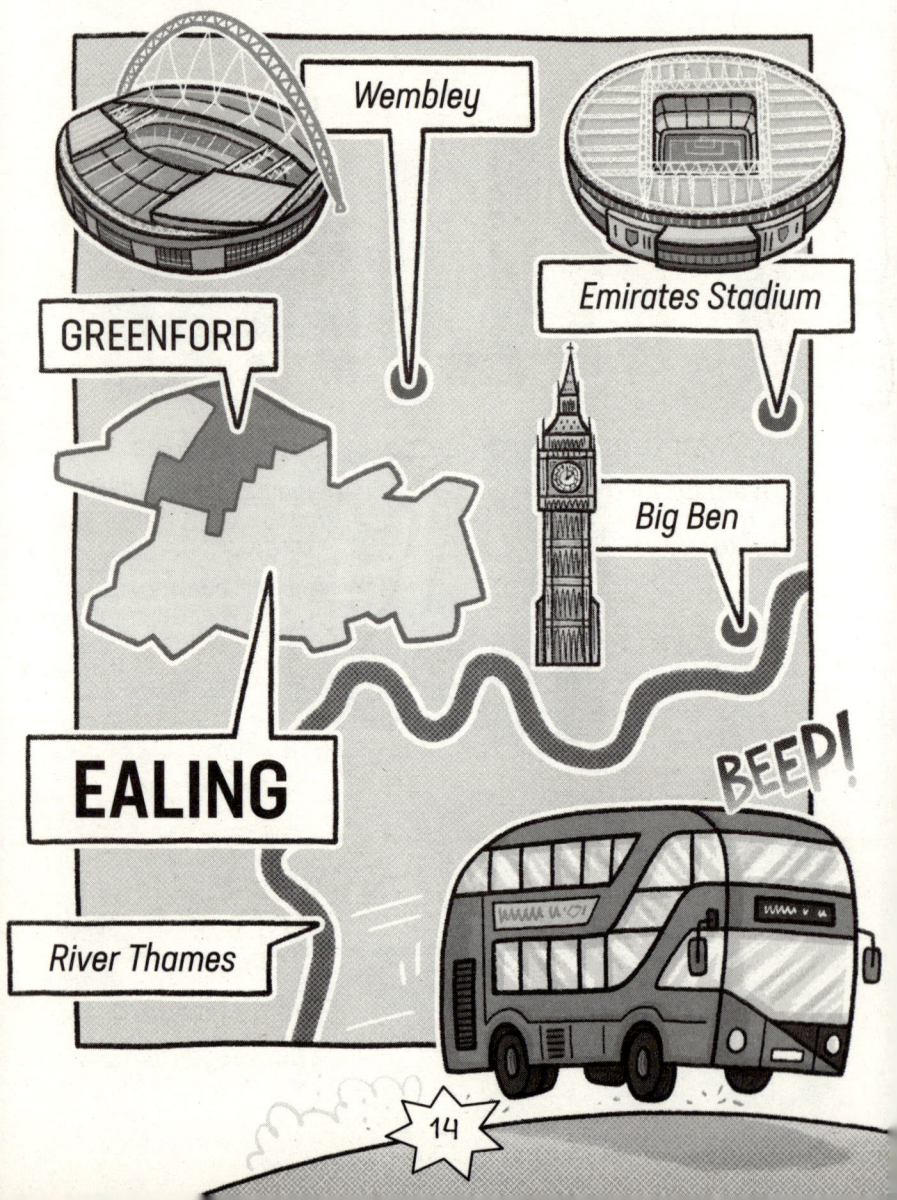

Ealing has been home to lots of other famous people, including:

**Peter Crouch**
*(very tall footballer)*

**Ada Lovelace**
*(pioneering computer programmer)*

**Martin Offiah**
*(rugby legend)*

**Freddie Mercury**
*(rock royalty)*

Bukayo's parents had moved to **London** from **Nigeria** in **West Africa** a few years before he was born.

Bukayo lived with his family in **Greenford**.

There was his mum, **Adeniki** . . .

Baby Bukayo

The Sakas are **Christians.** They regularly went to their local church as a family.

They followed God – and football, too!

Bukayo's dad is a **MASSIVE** Newcastle United fan.

*Alan Shearer* is Yomi's hero.

When Bukayo was eight, his dad took him to his first football match - **Manchester United** vs **Newcastle United** at **Old Trafford**.

As soon as they got home from school, **Bukayo** and **Abayomi** would be in the **garden** playing football.

When dad played with them, they put him in **goal**.

OI! WATCH MY FLOWERS!

OOPS!

They lost lots of balls over the **garden fence!**

When they were older, the brothers played on the **green** in front of their house with other kids from the street.

By the age of **six,** Bukayo's talent was beginning to show - and he loved playing football.

So, his dad took him along to their local club, **Greenford Celtic.**

The **coach** said that at the time the club were **not** taking on any new players.

But Bukayo's dad said:

JUST WATCH HIM PLAY...

22

And he did.

**WOW!** OKAY, WE'LL FIND A PLACE FOR HIM IN THE TEAM!

"I JUST USED TO PLAY EVERYWHERE ON THE PITCH... AND I WANTED TO SCORE GOALS."

*Bukayo on his time at Greenford Celtic*

Bukayo's brother **Abayomi** was a good

footballer, too.

While he was at the **Watford Academy**, Bukayo went with him.

**Jadon Sancho** was there at the same time and the three boys became friends.

Jadon would often come and **hang out** at home with the Sakas!

WOAH, GREAT MOVE JADON!

Bukayo went to the **Edward Betham Primary School** in Greenford.

He was the **star player** on the football team. The school won the **Ealing Peal Shield** (a local schools tournament) in **2012** and **2013**.

The school had never won the trophy before!

Bukayo visited his old school in **2022** to thank his teachers and meet the pupils.

The school has a **mural** of its superstar ex-pupil.

29

Lots of clubs sent **scouts** to watch Bukayo play at **Greenford Celtic.** As well as Watford, he had trials for **Tottenham** and **Chelsea.**

But when he was just **seven,** Bukayo and his family chose the club that would change his life . . .

It was all about football in the Saka house!

At weekends, Mum would take Abayomi

to **Watford** and Dad took Bukayo to the

**Arsenal Academy** at **Hale End.**

Bukayo spent a lot of

time in his Dad's car . . .

At **Greenford High School,** 11-year-old Bukayo was again the school team's top player.

They won **LOADS** of trophies with him. He was so good that his **PE teacher** sometimes took him off at half-time – just to give the other side a chance!

GOOD JOB BUKAYO!

Mr Harvey, Bukayo's PE teacher

Arsenal legend, and football pundit,

**Paul Merson** also went to **Greenford High School.**

# PAUL *MERSON*

ARSENAL **ICON**

POSITION: *FORWARD*

AT ARSENAL: *1985-1997*

APPEARANCES: *425*

GOALS: *99*

HONOURS: *2 x LEAGUE CHAMPION, 1 x FA CUP, 1 x LEAGUE CUP*

Football was **EVERYTHING** for Bukayo.

He played whenever he could, but that didn't

mean he forgot about his schoolwork.

Mum and Dad told him it was **VERY IMPORTANT** to get a good education. His teacher said he was a 'model pupil'.

He got excellent grades in his **GCSEs** - **FOUR A\*s** and **THREE As.**

Greenford High School is of course **VERY** proud of its former student who made it **BIG!**

"HE WAS ALWAYS SO HUMBLE... ONE DAY, HE'LL BE ARSENAL CAPTAIN."

*Mark Harvey, Bukayo's PE teacher at Greenford High School*

36

CHAPTER 4

# SAKA'S HEROES

# EVERYBODY LOVES RON

Every young footballer has their **heroes** when they're growing up.

For Bukayo, one of his biggest idols was...
**Cristiano Ronaldo.**

He and his friends would all copy Ronaldo's famous goal celebration.

Yessss!

Saka was just two years old when Ronaldo first signed for **Manchester United** in **2003.**

# GUNNERS *ICONS*

Bukayo's **FAVOURITE PLAYER OF ALL TIME** is . . . the one and only **Thierry Henry!**

ARSENAL **ICON**

KAPOW!

40

# THIERRY **HENRY**

POSITION: **STRIKER**

AT ARSENAL: **1999-2007, 2012**

APPEARANCES: **377**

GOALS: **228**

HONOURS: **2 x PREMIER LEAGUE,
2 x FA CUP**

When Saka was in the Arsenal Academy,

the Arsenal star he idolised most was

**Alexis Sanchez.**

"I WEAR THE SAME BOOTS AS SANCHEZ!"

"I'VE HAD A LOT OF HELP FROM DIFFERENT PLAYERS, BUT I'D SAY PROBABLY THE BIGGEST IMPACT IS DAVID LUIZ... HE'S DONE THE MOST FOR ME IN MY CAREER."

*Bukayo Saka*

Former Arsenal defender David Luiz helped Saka settle into the first team.

CHAPTER 5

# YOUNG GUNNER

Bukayo **soon stood** out in the academy at Arsenal. For such a young player, his **PACE** was **unbelievable** . . .

**ZOOM!**

He was **STRONG** and **CLEVER** . . .

**WHAM!**

And his **LEFT FOOT** was **fearsome!**

44

However, it was not all good. For a while Bukayo had **GROWING PAINS** that hurt his **ankles** and **knees**.

But he **LISTENED** to his coaches, trained hard, and quickly worked his way up through the age groups.

By the time Bukayo made it to the **under-15s,** he was becoming a major talent.

The under-15s coach was none other than **Freddie Ljungberg.** Bukayo could hardly believe it!

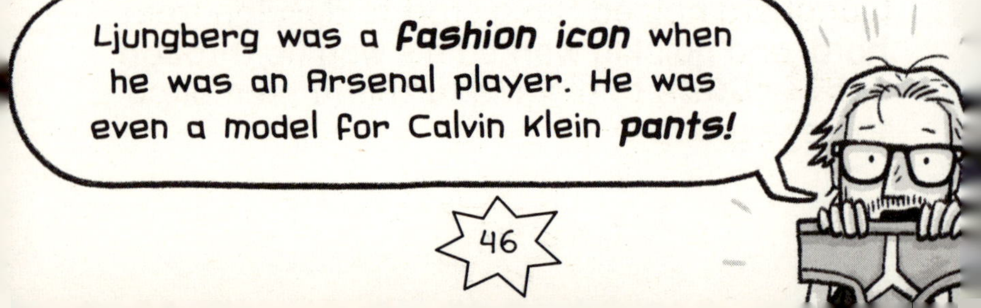

FWUMP!

Ljungberg was a **fashion icon** when he was an Arsenal player. He was even a model for Calvin Klein **pants!**

# FREDDIE LJUNGBERG

**ARSENAL ICON**

POSITION: **WINGER**

AT ARSENAL: **1998-2007**

APPEARANCES: **328**

GOALS: **72**

HONOURS: **2 x PREMIER LEAGUE, 3 x FA CUP**

Ljungberg helped Saka start to develop from a **left-back** to playing further up the pitch.

# UNDER-18s HIGHLIGHTS

## TEENAGE MAGIC MOMENTS

### 25 NOVEMBER 2017

*U18 PREMIER LEAGUE*

### ARSENAL U18 6-0 TOTTENHAM U18

*Saka scored the **first** and **third** goals as massive **North London** rivals Spurs were outgunned. Bukayo was taking off.*

### 16 MARCH 2018

*U18 PREMIER LEAGUE*

### NORWICH U18 0-4 ARSENAL U18

*Saka was in the **heart of the action,** scoring and quickly setting up another goal for a team-mate in this big away win.*

**25 AUGUST 2018**

*U18 PREMIER LEAGUE*

**ARSENAL U18 7-0 LEICESTER U18**

*Another **big, big** win for Saka - he scored **TWO** goals and provided **TWO** assists!*

In September 2018,

Saka signed his first

**PROFESSIONAL**

**CONTRACT** at Arsenal.

# UNDER-21 AND UNDER-23 HIGHLIGHTS

## 21 SEPTEMBER 2018

*PREMIER LEAGUE 2*

### ARSENAL U23 4-0 LIVERPOOL U23

*Saka scored his **first goal** at this level – and provided an assist for **Joe Willock.***

WHOMP!

## 7 NOVEMBER 2018

*EFL TROPHY*

### FOREST GREEN U21 1-3 ARSENAL U21

*Saka didn't score but he ran the show, setting up **two** of the **three** goals.*

## 14 JANUARY 2019

*PREMIER LEAGUE 2*

### ARSENAL U23 5-1 MAN CITY U23

*Our boy was **EXCELLENT** once again, scoring two goals as City were hammered.*

BOMP!

# LONDON BOYS

These Arsenal team-mates graduated around the same time as Saka...

## EDDIE NKETIAH

The South Londoner started at the Chelsea academy but crossed the capital to Arsenal when he was 16. The striker scored a memorable late winner in a 3-2 win over Manchester United in 2023.

# EMILE SMITH ROWE

Croydon-born Smith Rowe and Saka came through the academy together, now they're making magic in the first team!

# REISS NELSON

Nelson joined Arsenal as a nine-year old, then spent time on loan in Germany and the

Netherlands before returning to North London in 2022. Scored an absolute belter to win in the last minute against Bournemouth in March 2023.

# SAKA'S YOUTH RECORD

## UNDER-18

| SEASON | GAMES | GOALS | ASSISTS |
| --- | --- | --- | --- |
| 2017-18 | 22 | 8 | 5 |
| 2018-19 | 6 | 8 | 2 |

## UNDER-21/23

| SEASON | GAMES | GOALS | ASSISTS |
| --- | --- | --- | --- |
| 2018-19 | 24 | 6 | 10 |
| 2019-20 | 1 | – | – |

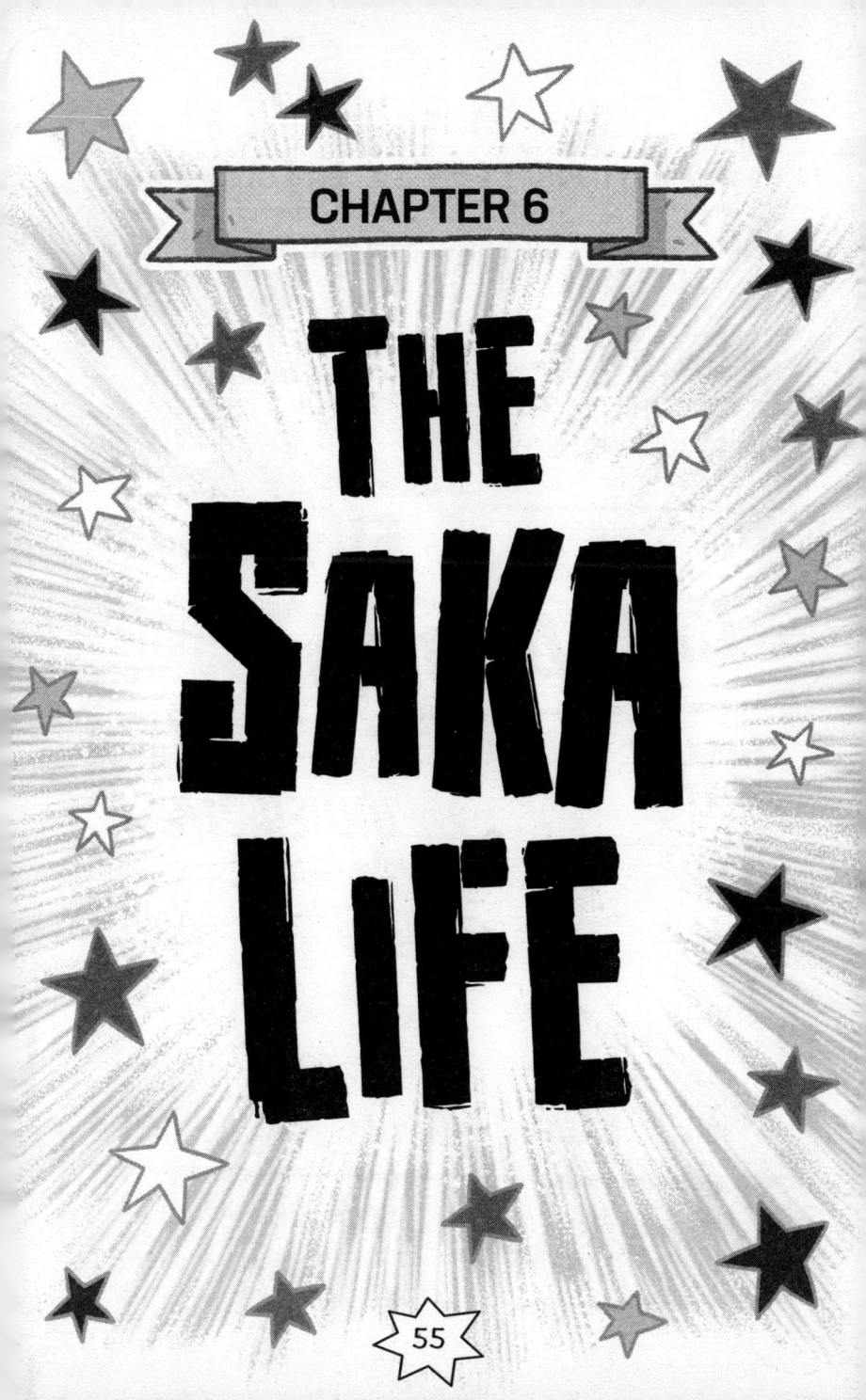

CHAPTER 6

# THE SAKA LIFE

Everybody needs to have a bit of downtime.

Saka uses his for some **serious gaming.**

He claims to be the best gamer at Arsenal.

His favourites are:

FIFA (of course)

CALL OF DUTY

GTA

NBA

Custom controller

He even has a *custom controller* given to him by his sponsor.

Bukayo has to have music with him wherever he goes...

# BOOM-TIK-T~~~H!
# TIK-TIS~~
# BOOM-T~

He's a massive fan of **AFROBEATS**.

Though he also likes **Ed Sheeran!**

COOL, THANKS BUKAYO!

TRACTOR BOYS FOREVER!

Ed is a massive **Ipswich Town** fan.

Saka has nearly **4 MILLION** followers on Instagram, where he uses the handle **GOD'S CHILD**.

Being a **Christian** is very important

to Bukayo. He takes his **Bible** with him everywhere (along with his games console) and prays every evening.

Bukayo is very close to his **family.** He lives with his mum and dad in a house near the Arsenal training ground.

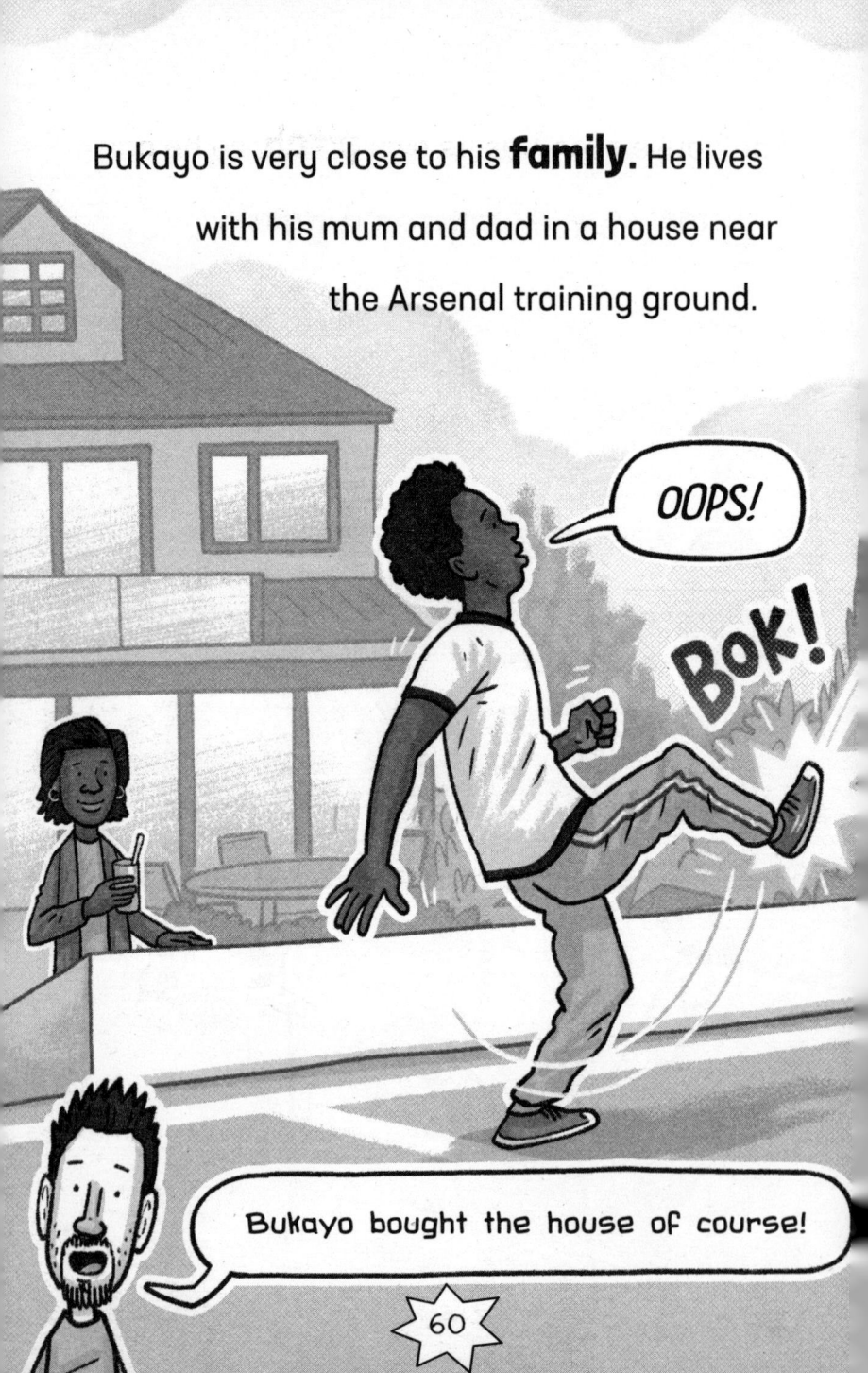

The house even has its own **pitch,** so he can still practise with his dad and brother.

OI! WATCH MY FLOWERS!

Bukayo and his family always remember their heritage in **Nigeria.**

Just before the **2022 World Cup** Bukayo worked with the BigShoe charity to help 120 children in the city of **Kano** in Nigeria have surgery that would change their lives.

CHAPTER 7

# YOUNG LION

While Bukayo was impressing his youth coaches at Arsenal, he was also making a name for himself with **ENGLAND.**

He quickly worked his way through the youth teams, and was playing for the **England Under-19s** when he made his senior Arsenal debut.

# 20 MARCH 2019

*EURO UNDER-19 QUALIFIER*

## ENGLAND U19 4-1 CZECH REPUBLIC U19

*Saka was on fire in this match at England's* **St George's Park** *base – scoring* **TWO GOALS** *and assisting another.*

CRACK!

And the England manager

**Gareth Southgate**

was watching!

# WEMBLEY DREAM

**1 OCTOBER 2020**

*INTERNATIONAL FRIENDLY*

**ENGLAND 3-0 WALES**

Gareth Southgate used this friendly to bring

in some new faces into the England squad.

They included **Dominic Calvert–Lewin,**

**Reece James** and of course, our man **Saka.**

Dominic Calvert-Lewin

66

Reece James

Bukayo was **incredibly honoured** to wear the **THREE LIONS** and to play under the famous **Wembley Arch** - just a few miles from where he grew up.

WOW!

The match was played *behind closed doors* because of the Covid pandemic.

# GOAL GETTER

**2 JUNE 2021**

*INTERNATIONAL FRIENDLY*

**ENGLAND 1-0 AUSTRIA**

Just before the delayed **EURO 2020** tournament, England played some warm-up matches at the **Riverside Stadium** in **Middlesbrough.**

Saka had been selected for the **EUROS** squad and was playing **in front of supporters** for the first time, as Covid restrictions were being relaxed.

So... what a moment for Saka to score his **first England goal!**

WHAM!

Saka is the **third** Arsenal teenager to score for England (after Theo Walcott and Alex Oxlade-Chamberlain)

69

"YOU DREAM OF THAT AS A KID, SCORING FOR YOUR COUNTRY, COMING THROUGH THE AGE GROUPS WITH ENGLAND SO TO DO IT HERE FOR THE SENIORS – IT'S AN AMAZING FEELING"

*- Bukayo Saka on his first goal for England.*

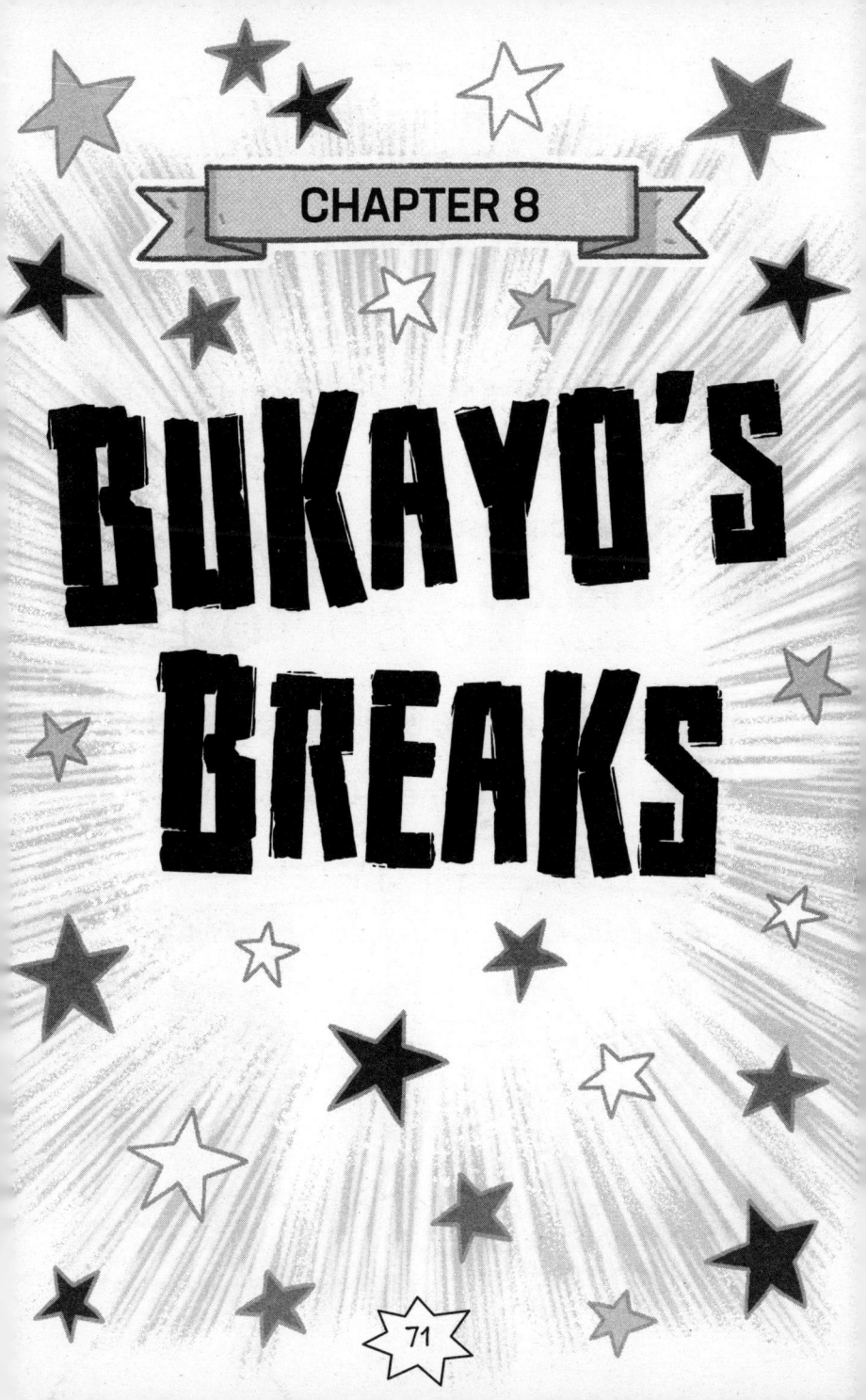

CHAPTER 8

# BUKAYO'S BREAKS

In **2018,** on a **FREEZING** November night in Ukraine, then Arsenal manager **Unai Emery** gave a 17-year-old Saka his first team **debut** against **Vorskla Poltava.**

**Emile Smith Rowe** and **Eddie Nketiah** were also involved in the 3-0 win.

Emile Smith Rowe

Eddie Nketiah

Two weeks later, Saka made his full home debut at the **Emirates Stadium** (in the Europa League again) in front of 60,000 fans.

SAKA WAS ON THE UP!

# NEW YEAR FIRSTS

## 1 JANUARY 2019

*PREMIER LEAGUE*

**ARSENAL 4-1 FULHAM**

It was a special start to **2019** for Saka. He had impressed his manager enough to earn a spot on the substitutes bench for this **Premier League** match against **Fulham.**

Bukayo was the first player born in **2001** to play in the Premier League.

The match was already won when Saka was

given the signal to warm up…

BUKAYO WAS A **PREMIER LEAGUE** PLAYER!

SAKA
87

He wore number **87** —
the highest number in
the Premier League.

# DREAM COME TRUE

**19 SEPTEMBER 2019**

*EUROPA LEAGUE*

**EINTRACHT FRANKFURT 0-3 ARSENAL**

Saka lined up alongside fellow young stars **Joe Willock** and **Emile Smith Rowe** for Arsenal's opening match in the **2019–20 Europa League.**

Joe Willock

Emile Smith Rowe

76

After a tricky start, Saka provided the assist for Willock's opener. And then, - **_BOOM_** - Saka scored himself - his **first senior Gunners** goal!

To cap his **MAN OF THE MATCH** performance, Saka set up **Pierre-Emerick Aubameyang** for the third.

A massive moment for Saka . . .

As the **2019–20** season went on, Saka became a **regular** in Arsenal's **starting line-up.**

He was doing well, but the team's results were not so good.

**Unai Emery** was **sacked** in November, and under-23s coach **Freddie Ljungberg** took charge for a few games.

In December, former Arsenal player
**Mikel Arteta** took over:

# MIKEL ARTETA

POSITION: **MIDFIELDER**

AT ARSENAL: **2011-2016**

APPEARANCES: **150**

GOALS: **16**

HONOURS: **2 x FA CUP**

# 2019-20 HIGHLIGHTS

## 27 JANUARY 2020

*FA CUP FOURTH ROUND*

### BOURNEMOUTH 1-2 ARSENAL

After an awesome team-move, Saka **fired the ball** into the net for a stunning finish – and **assisted Eddie Nketiah** for the second.

## 23 FEBRUARY 2020

*PREMIER LEAGUE*

### ARSENAL 3-2 EVERTON

*Arsenal had gone behind in the first minute, but Saka's **assist** for Eddie Nketiah's equaliser kickstarted their fightback in this **thriller** at the Emirates.*

## 4 JULY 2020

*PREMIER LEAGUE*

### WOLVES 0-2 ARSENAL

*Saka celebrated signing a new Arsenal contract by scoring his first **Premier League goal** with a sweet left-footed volley. **Beautiful stuff!***

Saka was on the bench for Arsenal's **FA Cup** win over Chelsea, but he'd done more than enough that season to **earn his medal.**

## SAKA'S *2019-20* RECORD

| GAMES | GOALS | ASSISTS |
|-------|-------|---------|
| 38 | 4 | 12 |

**Big things** were happening for Bukayo in the **2020–21 season . . .**

Arsenal beat **Premier League** champions **Liverpool** in a penalty shoot-out to win the **Community Shield.**

Saka (Arsenal's **leading assist-provider** in the previous season) had set up **Aubameyang's** goal.

He was now one of **Arsenal's most important players** - and capable of playing in almost any position in midfield.

THE **STARBOY** REALLY WAS **SHINING** . . .

On **Boxing Day 2020,** Saka's goal in a 3-1 win against Chelsea began a brilliant run of form that included **FOUR GOALS** and **TWO ASSISTS** in **SIX** Premier League matches.

As a result, he was voted **ARSENAL PLAYER OF THE MONTH** for **December, January,** and **February.**

After scoring in the Europa League quarter-final to beat **Slavia Prague** 4-0, Saka was named **Europa League Player of the Week.**

**THANK YOU!**

Saka capped a brilliant year as he was named **Arsenal Player of the Season 2020–21.**

# SAKA'S *2020-21* RECORD

| GAMES | GOALS | ASSISTS |
|:-----:|:-----:|:-------:|
| 46 | 7 | 10 |

# CHAPTER 10

# HEROES
## AND
## HEARTBREAK

**EURO 2020** finally started in June 2021. It was Saka's first major international tournament.

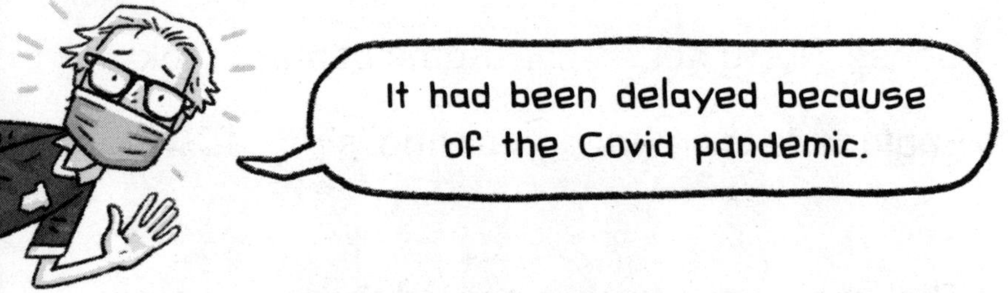

> It had been delayed because of the Covid pandemic.

Against the **Czech Republic,** Saka started the move that led to England's goal. It was another **man-of-the-match** performance that ended with a 1-0 win for England.

SUPERB!

WOMP!

In the **semi-final** against **Denmark,** his dangerous cross led to an own goal for the Danes. Harry Kane's extra-time penalty took England to their first major final since **1966.**

The whole country was behind the team – and Saka was **loving it.**

In the final, England were ahead after just **TWO MINUTES,** but by the time Saka came off the bench the score was 1-1.

And so to the penalty shoot-out . . . **Marcus Rashford** and **Jadon Sancho** had missed and it was down to **Bukayo** to keep England in it . . .

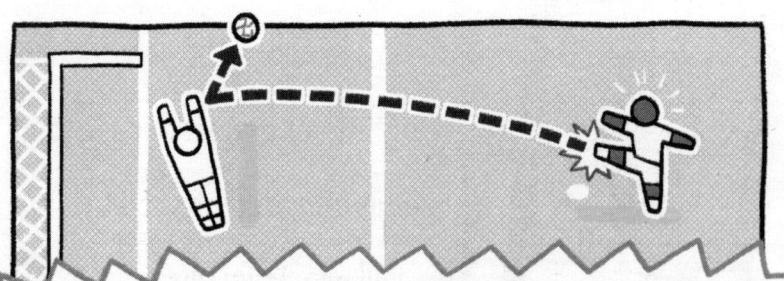

. . . **but his spot-kick was saved.**

**Gareth Southgate** hugged Saka as the country felt his pain.

Unfortunately, **Saka, Rashford** and **Sancho** received racist abuse on social media. Saka showed his class by the way he responded.

"There is no place for racism or hate of any kind in football or in any area of society... We will win. Love always wins."

# THE ROAD TO QATAR

Just two months after the EUROs, England resumed their qualifying campaign for the **2022 World Cup in Qatar. Bukayo** was involved for the first time.

He was a late sub in a **4–0** win against **Hungary,** but started against **Andorra,** scoring a goal and assisting **Jesse Lingard** in another **4–0** drubbing.

England secured qualification by hammering poor **San Marino 10–0,** with Saka again scoring and assisting.

# WORLD CUP HIGHLIGHTS

BUKAYO'S BEST BITS OF **QATAR 2022**

## 21 NOVEMBER 2022

*WORLD CUP GROUP B*

**ENGLAND 6-2 IRAN**

*Iran were totally outplayed by England in the group opener – as Saka scored **TWO GOALS.***

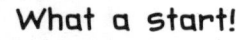

What a start!

## 4 DECEMBER 2022

*WORLD CUP ROUND OF 16*

**ENGLAND 3-0 SENEGAL**

*Saka was on the scoresheet again, as England overcame the Africa Cup of Nations champions and progressed to the quarter-final.*

# 10 DECEMBER 2022

*WORLD CUP QUARTER-FINAL*

## ENGLAND 1-2 FRANCE

*England were brilliant against the reigning champions and Saka's dangerous play in the box brought a penalty for **Harry Kane** and a chance for the Three Lions to equalise. Sadly, it wasn't England's day - **again!***

OH NO!

# SAKA'S ENGLAND RECORD

| GAMES | GOALS | ASSISTS |
|:-----:|:-----:|:-------:|
| 26 | 8 | 7 |

"IT'S REALLY IMPORTANT IN TOURNAMENT FOOTBALL TO HAVE A GREAT TEAM SPIRIT BECAUSE YOU CAN SEE THE QUALITY WE HAVE ON THE PITCH AND ALSO OFF THE PITCH."

*- Bukayo Saka*

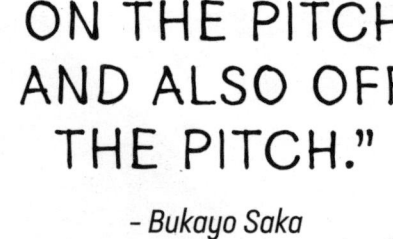

CHAPTER 11

RISING STARS

99

Saka is one of the **VERY BEST** young players in the world. Who else is up there with him?

# PEDRI

DATE OF BIRTH: **25 November 2002**

CLUB / COUNTRY: **Barcelona / Spain**

POSITION: **Midfielder**

ESTIMATED VALUE: **£87 million**

*Pedri's technique and vision earned him the Best Young Player Award at **EURO 2020** and the **Golden Boy** award in 2021. Barcelona's midfield magician shone again at the 2022 World Cup.*

Pedri is the youngest Spanish player to play at the **European Championship**.

# JUDE **BELLINGHAM**

DATE OF BIRTH: **29 June 2003**

CLUB / COUNTRY: **Borussia Dortmund / England**

POSITION: **Midfielder**

ESTIMATED VALUE: **£105 million**

*Jude went from the **Championship** with Birmingham to the **Champions League** with Borussia Dortmund in less than a year. He was outstanding for England at the 2022 World Cup and is tipped as a future captain for his country.*

Bellingham is the **youngest English player** to score in the **Champions League** (17 years 85 days).

# ERLING **HAALAND**

DATE OF BIRTH: **21 July 2000**

CLUB / COUNTRY: **Manchester City / Norway**

POSITION: **Striker**

ESTIMATED VALUE: **£148 million**

*Haaland is quite simply a goalscoring machine. Since moving from Borussia Dortmund, he has torn through the* **Premier League,** *leaving defences standing and breaking records for fun.*

Haaland took only SIX games to score **10 Premier League** goals – faster than any other player.

# ENZO FERNANDEZ

DATE OF BIRTH: **17 January 2001**

CLUB / COUNTRY: **Chelsea / Argentina**

POSITION: **Midfielder**

ESTIMATED VALUE: **£75 million**

*Fernandez won the **2022 World Cup** with Argentina just two months after making his international debut. The in-demand midfielder moved from River Plate in Argentina to Benfica in Portugal and then to Chelsea in just seven months.*

Fernandez was voted **Best Young Player** at the 2022 World Cup.

# PHIL **FODEN**

**DATE OF BIRTH:** **28 May 2000**

**CLUB / COUNTRY:** **Manchester City / England**

**POSITION:** **Midfielder**

**ESTIMATED VALUE:** **£97 million**

*Foden has been with City (the team he supports) since he was just* **FOUR.** *The gifted, intelligent midfielder is, like Saka, a danger all over the pitch and is key to England's future.*

Foden is the youngest winner of a **Premier League** medal.

# VINICIUS JUNIOR

DATE OF BIRTH: **12 July 2000**

CLUB / COUNTRY: **Real Madrid / Brazil**

POSITION: **Forward**

ESTIMATED VALUE: **£105 million**

*The Brazilian winger with electrifying pace is key to Real Madrid's devastating attacking line. His goals and assists in 2021-22 helped Madrid to **La Liga** and **Champions League** success.*

Junior scored the winning goal in the **2022 Champions League** final.

# ON THE *BENCH*

## RODRYGO

*REAL MADRID*
WINGER

## ALPHONSO DAVIES

*BAYERN MUNICH*
DEFENDER

## ALEJANDRO GARNACHO

*MANCHESTER UNITED*
WINGER

## GAVI

*BARCELONA*
MIDFIELDER

## JAMAL MUSIALA

*BAYERN MUNICH*
MIDFIELDER

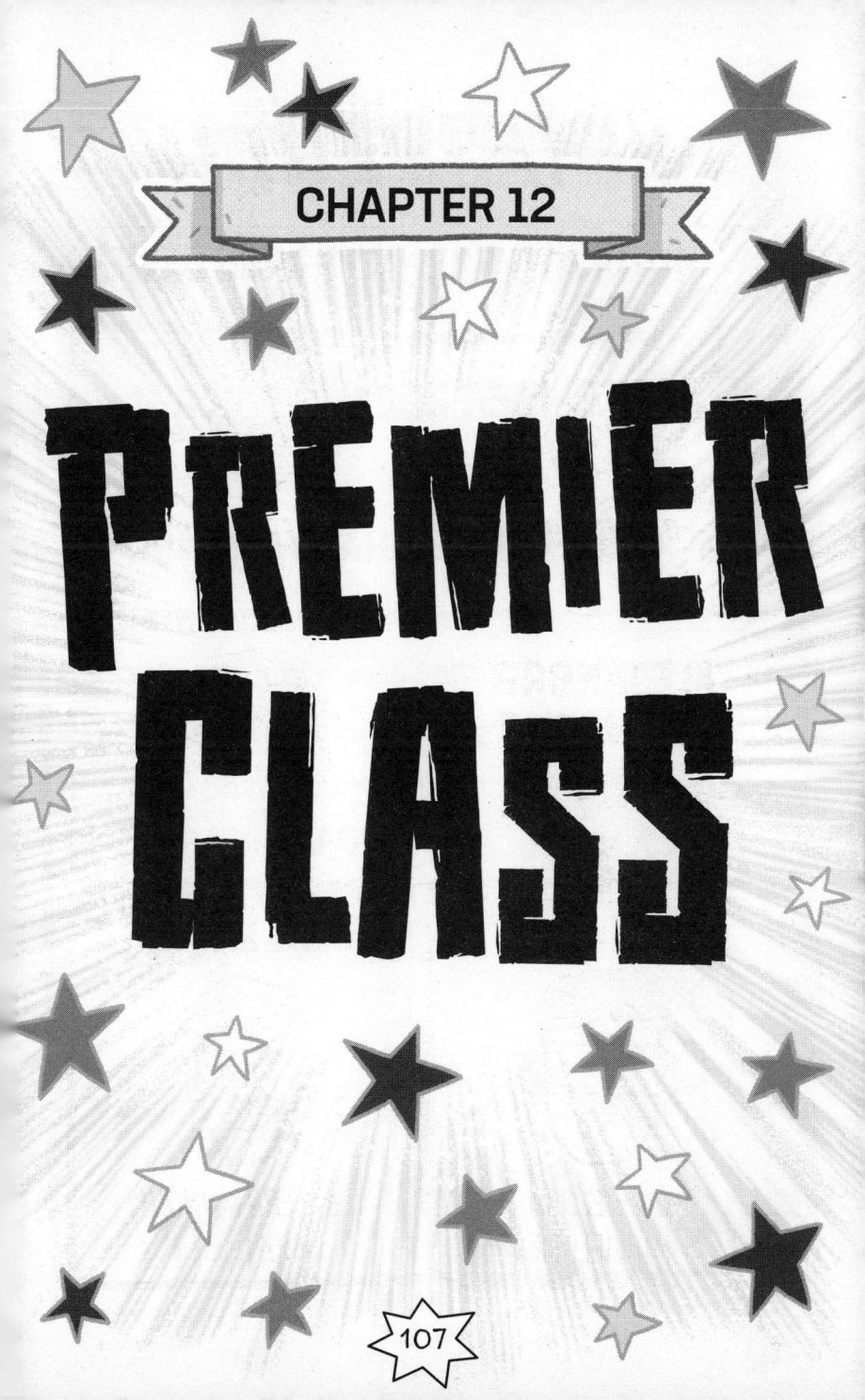

CHAPTER 12

PREMIER CLASS

# HIGHLIGHTS 2021-22

THE BEST BITS OF ANOTHER
BIG SEASON FOR SAKA...

## 26 SEPTEMBER 2021

*PREMIER LEAGUE*

### ARSENAL 3-1 TOTTENHAM HOTSPUR

*Arsenal suffered three straight league defeats at the beginning of the season, but they were picking up points by the time they faced their north London rivals.*

*Saka's **GOAL** and **ASSIST** for **Emile Smith Rowe** secured a **MASSIVE** win.*

WHAM!

# 26 DECEMBER 2021

*PREMIER LEAGUE*

## NORWICH CITY 0-5 ARSENAL

*Saka put the Gunners ahead after just **SIX** minutes and then scored the third as Norwich were well-beaten in this Boxing Day thrashing. The perfect Christmas gift!*

Saka's second strike against Norwich was his **tenth goal** for Arsenal.

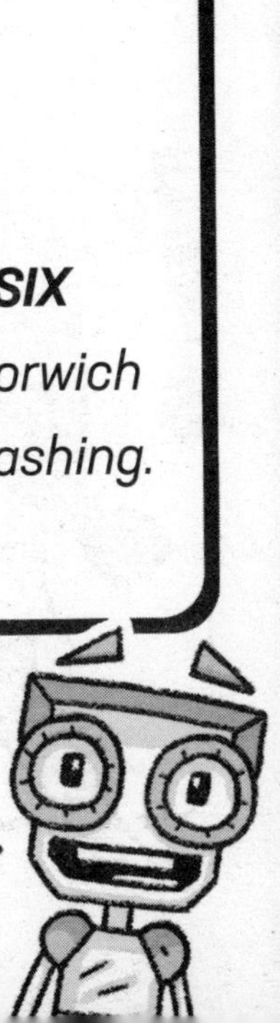

Saka's awesome form continued for the
**2021–22 season . . .**

POW!!

He scored important goals in BIG wins against
**Chelsea** and **Manchester United . . .**

110

. . . and finished as Arsenal's top scorer, with **12 GOALS** in all competitions.

His top performances saw him named **Arsenal Player of the Season** for the second year in a row.

Saka was the first player to do that since **Thierry Henry** nearly 20 years' before!

Bukayo and fellow Arsenal academy graduate **Emile Smith Rowe** were becoming standout stars in this exciting young team.

The fans came up with brilliant chant to the tune of **'Rockin' All Over the World'** by 70s rockers **Status Quo . . .**

HERE WE GO, OH! ROCKIN' ALL OVER THE WORLD.

# HIGHLIGHTS 2022-23

## 9 OCTOBER 2022

*PREMIER LEAGUE*

### ARSENAL 3-2 LIVERPOOL

**Two goals** from Bukayo, including the winner scored from the spot, helped Arsenal claim top spot in the Premier League.

FWOMP!

## 22 JANUARY 2023

*PREMIER LEAGUE*

### ARSENAL 3-2 MANCHESTER UNITED

*The Gunners were flying, on a **12-game** unbeaten Premier League run, when Saka scored against United in another **thrilling win.***

## 18 FEBRUARY 2023

*PREMIER LEAGUE*

### ASTON VILLA 2-4 ARSENAL

*Villa took an early lead, but Bukayo's **equaliser** helped inspire the comeback that ended with an convincing away **win.***

The season was Arsenal's **finest** for many years. They topped the league for weeks and looked to be on target for their first **Premier League title** since 2003-04.

And Saka was the beating heart of the team's attacking play.

Unfortunately, a late-season dip in form allowed *Manchester City* to snatch the title from Bukayo and the Gunners.

All season long, opponents were terrified of Bukayo's **speed** and **skill** and would do anything to stop him . . .

CRUNCH!

HE ENDED THE SEASON WITH HIS BEST EVER PREMIER LEAGUE STATS – **14 GOALS** AND **11 ASSISTS**.

# ARSENAL LEGENDS SPEAK

Some of the greatest Gunners on

## Starboy Saka . . .

"AFTER MISSING THAT PENALTY [AT THE EUROS], HE'S NEVER LOOKED BACK SINCE..."

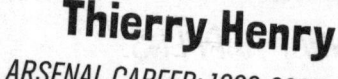

**Thierry Henry**
*ARSENAL CAREER: 1999-2007, 2012*

"IF THERE'S A BETTER PLAYER IN WORLD FOOTBALL AT THE MOMENT . . . THE ONLY ONE I CAN THINK OF IS LIONEL MESSI."

**Tony Adams**
ARSENAL CAREER: 1983-2002

"HE IS THE ONE PLAYER WHO WOULD WALK INTO THE 2003-04 INVINCIBLES TEAM."

**Martin Keown**
ARSENAL CAREER: 1985-86, 1993-2004

"HE WILL ALWAYS BE OUR STARBOY NO MATTER WHAT HAPPENS."

**Ian Wright**
ARSENAL CAREER: 1991-98

Bukayo is a young player at the beginning of his career, but he's already proved himself to be **ESSENTIAL** for club and country.

As fans, we can look forward to enjoying his **super skills,** winning smile and fantastic attitude for **years to come** . . .

# QUIZ TIME!

How much do you know about **BUKAYO SAKA?** Try this quiz to find out, then test your friends!

**1.** Where was Bukayo born?

------------------------------------------------

**2.** Which team does his dad support?

------------------------------------------------

**3.** Which footballer did Bukayo and his brother know when they were kids?

------------------------------------------------

**4.** How many A* GCSEs did Bukayo get at school?

------------------------------------------------

**5.** Which Arsenal legend was Saka's under-15s coach?

------------------------------------------------

**6.** What is Saka's Instagram handle?

------------------------------------------------

**7.** Against which team did Saka score his first England goal?

------------------------------------------------

**8.** Which team did Arsenal beat in the 2020 Community Shield?

------------------------------------------------

**9.** How many goals did Bukayo score against Iran at the 2022 World Cup?

------------------------------------------------

**10.** Arsenal fans have a chant about Saka and which other player?

------------------------------------------------

The answers are on the next page *but no peeking!*

# ANSWERS

1. Greenford, Ealing, west London

2. Newcastle United

3. Jadon Sancho

4. Four

5. Freddie Ljungberg

6. God's Child

7. Austria

8. Liverpool

9. Two

10. Emile Smith Rowe

# BUKAYO SAKA:
## *WORDS YOU SHOULD KNOW*

### Premier League
The top football league in England.

### PFA
Professional Footballers' Association.

### World Cup
The biggest tournament for national teams.

### FA Cup
The top English knockout cup competition.

### Europa League
The second-tier European club competition.

### EUROs
The European Championship – Europe's main national team competition.

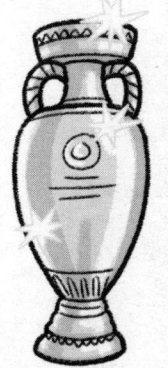

# HAVE YOU READ ANY OF THESE OTHER BOOKS FROM THE SUPERSTARS SERIES?

## FOOTBALL SUPERSTARS

**16** FOOTBALL SUPERSTARS
**ZLATAN** RULES
·FACTS·STORIES·STATS·
SIMON MUGFORD ★ DAN GREEN

**17** FOOTBALL SUPERSTARS
**HAALAND** RULES
·FACTS·STORIES·STATS·
SIMON MUGFORD ★ DAN GREEN

**18** FOOTBALL SUPERSTARS
**MARTENS** RULES
·FACTS·STORIES·STATS·
SIMON MUGFORD ★ DAN GREEN

**19** FOOTBALL SUPERSTARS
**BRONZE** RULES
·FACTS·STORIES·STATS·
SIMON MUGFORD ★ DAN GREEN

**20** FOOTBALL SUPERSTARS
**LEWANDOWSKI** RULES
·FACTS·STORIES·STATS·
SIMON MUGFORD ★ DAN GREEN

**21** FOOTBALL SUPERSTARS
**GREALISH** RULES
·FACTS·STORIES·STATS·
SIMON MUGFORD ★ DAN GREEN

**22** FOOTBALL SUPERSTARS
**FOOTBALL RULES THE WORLD**
INCREDIBLE STORIES FROM THE BIGGEST GAME ON THE PLANET
SIMON MUGFORD ★ DAN GREEN

**23** FOOTBALL SUPERSTARS
**ENGLAND** RULE
·FACTS·STORIES·STATS·
SIMON MUGFORD ★ DAN GREEN

FOOTBALL SUPERSTARS
**FOOTBALL JOKES** RULE

FOOTBALL SUPERSTARS
**FOOTBALL QUIZZES** RULE

# COLLECT THEM ALL!

## SPORTS SUPERSTARS

SPORTS SUPERSTARS
**HAMILTON** RULES
·FACTS·STORIES·STATS·
SIMON MUGFORD ★ DAN GREEN

**2** SPORTS SUPERSTARS
**RADUCANU** RULES
·FACTS·STORIES·STATS·
SIMON MUGFORD ★ DAN GREEN

# MORE COMING SOON!

# ABOUT THE AUTHORS

**Simon's** first job was at the Science Museum, making paper aeroplanes and blowing bubbles big enough for your dad to stand in. Since then he's written all sorts of books about the stuff he likes, from dinosaurs and rockets, to llamas, loud music and of course, football. Simon has supported Ipswich Town since they won the FA Cup in 1978 (it's true - look it up) and once sat next to Rio Ferdinand on a train. He lives in Kent with his wife and daughter, a dog and a cat.

**Dan** has drawn silly pictures since he could hold a crayon. Then he grew up and started making books about stuff like trucks, space, people's jobs, *Doctor Who* and *Star Wars*. Dan remembers Ipswich Town winning the FA Cup but he didn't watch it because he was too busy making a Viking ship out of brown paper. As a result, he knows more about Vikings than football. Dan lives in Suffolk with his wife, son, daughter and a dog that takes him for very long walks.